Rags to Riches!
A modern Cinderella Story

Let's Make a
MOVIE

Kath Smith

Illustrated by
Emma Dodd

Hugh McIntosh   Jake Lang   Miranda Katz   Taro Tanaka   Mira Seth

MAKING A MOVIE takes a lot of people, time and money! Anyone who wants to make one needs to have an idea, put together a team of people to produce it – from stars to technicians – and then find someone who will invest money in the project. *Rags to Riches!* is a novel based on the Cinderella story – meet some of the key people and follow their progress as they go about making this book into a blockbuster movie.

HUGH McINTOSH, the **Producer,** deals with money, ideas and organisation. He has the original idea for this project and sets everything in motion. He looks for the best talent he can afford to make the film a success. Everything depends on him.

JAKE LANG, the **Director,** has the main creative job. He organises all the technicians, the creative people and all the props and scenery needed to turn his vision into reality.

MIRANDA KATZ, the **Script Writer,** has the job of re-writing the novel as a film script. She has to think about how the story, the characters and the action will work best on screen.

TARO TANAKA, the **Composer,** writes the music for the movie. This is called the score. It adds atmosphere and helps make certain scenes more moving or exciting.

MIRA SETH is the **Production Manager.** She's the Producer's assistant and her job is to solve the day-to-day problems that come up during filming. She prepares the budget and the filming schedule, hires equipment and technicians and draws up their contracts.

JULES FLYNN, the **First Assistant Director,** helps the Director with administration, budgets, schedules and general organisation. He has to make sure the actors know when they are needed on set and check that the technicians are doing their jobs properly.

Jules Flynn   Nathalie Archer   Morris Carver   Kyri Petros   Cory Little

NATHALIE ARCHER is the **Production Designer.** Her job is to create the look and mood of the movie. She designs the sets and chooses the props and the costumes.

MORRIS CARVER, the **Director of Continuity,** makes sure that nothing is out of place during the filming of different scenes and that all the action happens in the right order in the movie.

KYRI PETROS, the **Director of Photography,** supervises lighting and camera angles to provide the movie's visual mood. He is in charge of the Camera Crew.

CORY LITTLE, the **Sound Designer,** creates, mixes and edits the sound track to match the pictures and create the atmosphere the Director wants. He is in charge of the Sound Crew – the technicians who record and mix sound during filming.

JALEESA MARSHALL, the **Special Effects Manager,** works on computers and uses models to create all the special effects.

ANNA JONES, the **Casting Director,** works with the Director to find the right actors for all the roles in the film.

SANDRO FRAZZINI, the **Locations Manager,** searches for the best locations then gets permission to use them. He has to inform the police, local authorities etc. and after filming is over, it is his job to make sure everything is left as it was found.

KATY FLOWERS, the **Costume Designer,** researches, designs and creates the costumes.

LARRY PARKER is in charge of **Make-up** and hair dressing, to make the actors look the part.

SUSAN FIGGIS, the **Editor,** chooses and edits the best shots so the film has a good pace and atmosphere, according to the Director's vision.

Everyone has an assistant to help get everything done on time!

Contents

EVERY FILM STARTS in the same way – someone has a good idea! That person is usually a film producer who either works for a film studio or for himself. This is the story of how our Producer, Hugh McIntosh, turns his good idea into a blockbusting movie!

Hugh McIntosh has a good idea. "This book would make a fantastic movie!" He calls Film Director Jake Lang and asks him. "What do ya think, Jake? A fairy tale for the new millennium!"

"It's a winner, Hugh! I can see it now – *Rags to Riches!* starring Melody Winter as Cinders and Chuck Kerr as the Prince. I love it!"

Jake and Hugh
call Melody and
Chuck's agent with a proposal.
"Sounds interesting, Hugh. Let them read the book."

Hugh contacts the author who wrote the story, and
arranges to buy an option on the book for a year.
If the film is not made in that time, he will have to
pay even more money. Then he contacts Miranda
Katz who will make the book into a screenplay.
He gets in touch with a composer, Taro Tanaka,
whom he hopes will write the music for the film.

The film will cost millions of pounds to produce,
so Hugh starts the search for people who might want
to invest money to help pay for it. These investors
will take a large share of any
profit the film makes – that's the money the film
earns from ticket sales to people like you and I,
after everyone who worked on it has been paid.

Getting the Team Together

Producer Hugh McIntosh has been working very hard to plan a timetable for filming, to put together a budget, and to raise the money for his movie. Finally, things are starting to come together.

Today, Hugh has arranged a meeting with Minty Chocs and Smith & Wazir, two companies who are interested in investing in the film. He is going to present them with the 'package', which includes the stars, the director, the script and a budget.

There is an air of great excitement as they sit down to talk business.

"We must start filming in October," Hugh explains. "Any later and we'll have to extend the option on the book, and that will be costly."

"That's perfect timing," reply the investors. "The film can be released for the following Christmas. It should be very successful at the box-office."

Smith & Wazir head a consortium of investors who promise twelve million pounds if Hugh can get teenage heart throb, Miles Denne, on board to star as Buttons. Minty Chocs agree to invest a hundred thousand pounds, as long as stars are shown eating one of their chocolate bars in the movie.

Script Writer Miranda Katz has been putting together ideas for the script. She, Hugh, Jake and Nathalie Archer, the Production Designer, present what they have come up with so far. They show the investors rough storyboards so that they can get an idea of what happens in every scene.

The investors are delighted. Work can really begin now.

Hugh employs Production Manager Mira Seth to hire all the necessary people for the film. It is also Mira's job to hire all the filming equipment, sort out all the contracts, keep an eye on how much money is spent and plan the daily schedules for filming. She's a very busy person!

One of her first jobs will be to set up auditions with acting hopefuls. She must also find builders and technicians to start work on the set straightaway.

Casting

The lead actors are in place, the team must now fill the remaining roles. Casting Director, Anna Jones, helps Jake to choose – they see lots and lots of hopefuls, but not everyone is suitable.

Teenage heart throb, Miles Denne, has been persuaded to join the acting team, but the main lead Chuck Kerr is not happy. "I'm not sharing a dressing room with that little squirt! He's practically still in nappies!"

Fortunately, nobody hears what he says because Bang! Crash! Bang! it is very noisy and hectic in the Studio. Work is going on day and night to finish the main set on schedule, ready for filming next week.

Production Designer Nathalie Archer has built a scale model. Even the furniture is built in miniature. Nathalie watches anxiously as her plans become reality. Everywhere, designers, set painters, and skilled crafts people are measuring, painting, hammering and sawing.

The Props Department has hired or built all the furniture needed to fill the set. Now they are arranging it using Nathalie's plans as a guide. The Sound and Costume Designer are also on set. They have come to discuss ideas with Nathalie.

Filming Begins

It is the first day of filming and Jake is very excited. He has spent many weeks discussing his ideas with all the team. Now he is confident everyone knows what he wants, and that together they can begin to create his vision.

Kyri Petros has worked on a camera script with Jake. This script, along with finished storyboards, explains all the lighting details and tells the camera operators where they should be, which lenses to use, and how to move the equipment.

It is the job of the Sound Crew to record and create the kind of sound track Jake wants. The Boom Operator controls a microphone on the end of a long arm to pick up the sound. This sound must be carefully matched with the pictures.

Several cameras will film at once from different angles, to get the best possible shot. The camera assistants load film, focus lenses and keep the cameras running smoothly.

Jules Flynn, the First Assistant Director, checks his notes nervously. He needs to speak to Morris Carver, the Director of Continuity. But Morris is too busy gazing at Melody to pay any attention.

Tension is high on set.
Costume Designer Katy
Flowers, is trying to persuade Melody to wear her dress, while Chuck has another argument with Miles. "Lines on the face are a sign of... er, character, Chuck," soothes make-up artist, Larry Parker.

"Places, everyone!" calls Jake over the megaphone. Filming is about to begin.

Action!

"Action!" The cameras roll!

They are filming the scene from the middle of the story when the Prince asks Cinders to dance. Jake wants to create a magical, romantic atmosphere, so the set is flooded with soft lighting. Cinders is seated on a couch under an open window.

"Melody always looks wonderful," sighs Morris.

Artificial moonlight floods in and the camera zooms to capture her expression as the Prince approaches. The boom swings round, out of sight of the camera.

"Would you like to dance?" begins the Prince...

"Cut!" cries Jake. "Melody darling! He's asking you to dance, not jump off a bridge..."

Jake spends some time talking to Melody, to help her understand what he wants. In the meantime, Larry carefully retouches Chuck's make-up, and a wardrobe assistant brushes down his costume.

Composer Taro Tanaka is also on set today, looking for ideas. He is an important member of the creative team – his music will be a powerful tool for creating mood and atmosphere.

Looking at the Rushes

Every evening after shooting Jake meets with Kyri and the camera crew, the lighting technicians,

Susan Figgis, the film editor, Mira, Jules, Nathalie and Morris from Continuity to look at the filming they have done that day – the rushes.

Everyone watches the rushes keenly, anxious to see if the day's work was successful.

Jake is extremely pleased with the results. The lighting and mood is good, and the scene has turned out even better than he imagined it would. Suddenly, Morris pipes up.

"Melody's earrings have changed since the last shoot!"

Jake is furious. The scene will have to be shot again. He instructs Jules to have a word with the Wardrobe Department about the earrings. Someone is going to be in a lot of trouble! Mira is angry, too. Every delay costs time and money. The backers won't be pleased if they go over budget.

19

On Location

Before filming began, Location Manager Sandro Frazzini spent many months searching for the perfect place to film those scenes that are not shot in the studio.

Today the crew are filming the scene where the Fairy Godmother turns the pumpkin into a sports car. Sandro has hired out the grounds of a huge house, but the owners will only let them shoot there for one day. The film crew cannot afford to make any mistakes.

The scene takes place at dusk, so everyone has been waiting for the sun to go down. As the light begins to fade, the actors take their positions. Suddenly, it starts to rain.

They can't film in the rain, so everyone has to wait. But, by the time it stops raining, it is dark. After a short discussion with Mira, Kyri and the Film Crew, Jake makes a decision. "We're already over budget, and we just can't afford any more delays," he announces. "We'll have to film in the dark."

In the studio, sound and light can be closely controlled and the set carefully designed so that the director can get the best camera angles. But here, outside, anything can happen and Jake needs the Film Crew, especially the Lighting Technicians, to use all their skills to make the best of the situation.

Off set, one of the sound technicians is recording the wildtrack – background noise which will be added to the sound track later.

21

Special Effects!

Some action in the film is created by Jaleesa Marshall from the Special Effects Department. She and her team use a mixture of detailed models, specialised filming techniques and computers to create a host of amazing moments.

Jake wanted the Fairy Godmother to fly. To create this illusion, she was filmed in a flying position in the studio. The background was shot on another piece of film. Jaleesa scanned these two pieces of film into a powerful computer. Then she cut bits out of one and added them to the other, to create one picture – the Fairy Godmother flying.

The pumpkin was turned into a sports car on film using a computer technique called morphing. The sparkles were added on computer, too.

It would have cost a lot of money to film the crowd scene at the end of the film. Instead, a small group of extras was filmed in lots of different positions. These shots were then repeated and patched together seamlessly on computer, to create an enormous crowd.

The Make-up Department used a variety of techniques to make the Ugly Sisters as unattractive as possible. Hours of hard work, foam latex rubber, make-up and creativity went into constructing their ugly faces.

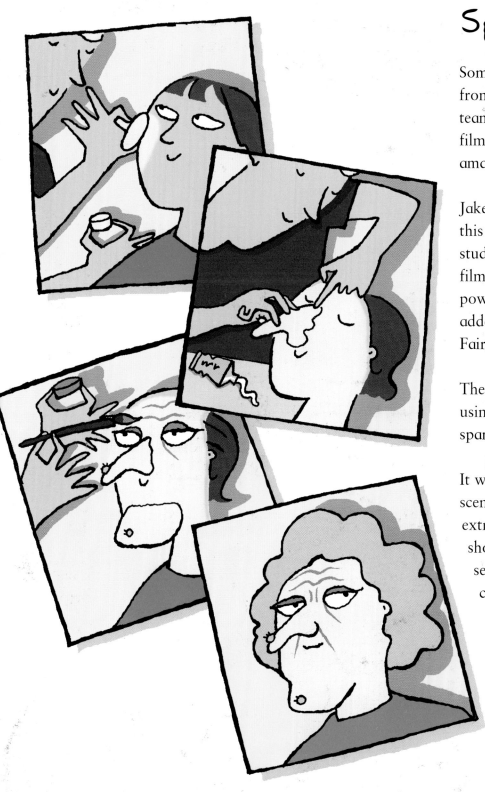

The Cutting Room

Film Editor Susan Figgis has the important job of putting together the final film. Editing begins as soon as the first day's shooting is done. The rushes from each day's filming are sent to her workshop – the cutting room – where she pieces them together on the editing table.

Susan watches the reels of film on her screen and listens to the sound tapes on a speaker. She chooses all the best bits, and then joins them together.

When all the cuts are more or less in the right order, she begins the difficult task of trimming and shaping the film. The final version is called the fine cut. Although Susan makes most of the decisions, Hugh and Jake have the final say on which cuts are used. The stars of the film like to have their say, too.

Sometimes the stars have to re-record some of their lines because the sound quality is not good enough. They stand in front of a screen and speak their lines as the film runs, taking care to match the movement of their lips with the screen images.

The Sound Track

After the film has been edited, it is time to add Composer Taro Tanaka's music.

Taro has spent many weeks composing music which will help set the mood, increase the tension and heighten the emotion. Today he is inputting the music onto a very complex computer. Once it has been input, it can be mixed and edited.

This will be done by Sound Engineer Cory Little.

Cory is in charge of mixing in all the special sound effects, such as the wildtrack. This is done in a studio on a sound desk. There are buttons on the desk for all the different sounds. Using them, Cory can fade sound in and out, balancing it to get just the right mix. It is a very skilled job.

Sound dubbing editors work on the edited sound track, to perfect the mix of words, sound effects and music, and to blend it perfectly with the pictures. They must also get rid of any unwanted noises, such as an aeroplane flying overhead.

The World Premiere

Before the film's release, it was shown to the Board of Censors, who awarded it a U certificate. This means that it is suitable for people of all ages. It was also shown to small audiences. These 'previews' were used to find out if the film will be successful.

Huge amounts of money have been spent on publicity by the Publicity Company, Starburst. Glossy posters showing Melody, Chuck and Miles are on every street corner. Hugh and Jake have been interviewed in magazines, the papers and on television. Trailers have been appearing in cinemas for weeks, tantalising the public with scenes from the film. There are even *Rags to Riches!* T-shirts for sale.

Finally the big night has arrived when the movie is shown in full for the first time at its World Premiere. The foyer is swarming with famous people, film critics and the press. All the team are there, too, nervously waiting to hear what the audience thinks of the film.

Jake spots Chuck and Melody getting out of a limo. "They make a lovely couple," he remarks to Hugh. "And they're still friends!"

"Hey! That gives me a great idea!" cries Hugh. "Cinderella, the sequel. How the happy couple get on after they're married. What do ya think?"

The Film Crew and Their Jobs

Lots and lots of people work on a film, apart from the main organisers we've already mentioned. Read the descriptions of these different jobs and see if you can find any of the people who do this work in the pictures!

Photography

Director of Photography
The Director of Photography manages a large team of people known as the Camera Crew. They include all sorts of technicians who work the cameras to make sure the picture is of the best possible quality and the atmosphere of the film is right.

Camera Operators
The Camera Operators work the cameras under the Director of Photography's directions. If there is any filming outside the studio, the Cam Remote operates the camera.

Focus Puller
The Focus Puller makes sure the picture is in focus. Camera lenses are made of different parts and kinds of lenses which help make the focusing smooth.

Clapper-loader
The Clapper-loader loads film into the magazine and holds up a slate at the beginning of each shot to keep track of what scene is being filmed and what 'take' it is. Some scenes have to be shot many times over to get them right. When the film is edited the best 'take' is chosen.

Grips
The Grips push the dolly (the tripod the camera stands on) and cranes holding overhead cameras. They also carry any other camera equipment around.

Other jobs include cleaning the lenses on the camera so that no bits of fluff or dust appear on the picture, looking after all the camera equipment, keeping records...

Lighting

Chief Lighting Technician
The Chief Lighting Technician oversees the Lighting Crew and works closely with the Director of Photography to make sure the sets are lit to give the best results.

Lighting Crew
Lots of different sorts of lights are used on set to give different effects. It is important that the lighting technicians know what scene is going to be filmed next and what sort of lighting will be needed. That way they can be ready in advance and avoid any long delays.

Gaffer
As well as people working the lights, there are electricians, chief of which is the Gaffer. His assistants are called Best Boys or Girls. The Rigging Gaffer sets up the lights in the rigging (the loft in a studio or theatre where the lights are).

Sound

Sound Designer
The Sound Crew work under the Sound Designer, to make sure the sound matches the pictures and creates the right atmosphere.

Boom Operator
The Boom Operator works the overhead microphone which is on the end of a long pole. The microphone must be near the actors, but must not be in front of the cameras.

Sound Recordist
The Sound Recordist records the dialogue (the actors speaking). He has to make sure there is no background noise disturbing the voices.

Foley Artist

Foley Artists match sound effects to the picture. For example, they may make the noise of someone walking down a gravel path.

Foley Mixer

The Foley Mixer is a sound engineer, whose job is to mix all the sound tracks together. These include the dialogue, the wildtrack (background hum behind the dialogue) and the ambient sound (the background sound of a particular location – for example bird song and wind in the wood, or people chatting and walking around at a party).

Sets, Props, Costumes, Make-up

Production Designer

The Production Designer designs the set.
She oversees the construction workers who build the sets and work closely with the Props, Wardrobe and Make-up Departments.

Construction Workers

They build the set. They are led by a foreman, and include builders, carpenters, electricians etc.

Props Department

The job of the Props Department is to furnish the set. They search for the right kind of furniture that matches the period in history the film is set in, and the kind of story. These items are called props, short for properties – anything the organisers have to buy or make for the film!

Wardrobe Department

The Wardrobe Staff work for the Costume Designer. They help make or find the costumes and are on hand throughout the filming to dress, press, mend and keep the costumes in order.

Make-up and Hairdressing Department

The Make-up Artists and Hairdressers are on hand to make the actors look the part. Sometimes it can take two or three hours to prepare an actor or actress. During filming they may mess up their hair or face and need to be quickly tidied up.

Post-production

Once the filming is over, the movie goes into post-production. This is when it is edited and the sound track is added.

Editor

The Editor has all sorts of technicians working for her who make sure the sound is of the best quality and fits perfectly with the pictures. There are also people who work on the special effects and make sure the picture quality is good.

Finance and legal teams

Accountants

The Accountants keep a check on the money: how much is spent, how it is spent, is everything on budget and so on.

Lawyers

The Lawyers make sure everyone has contracts that set the terms of their work (what they are expected to do and how much they will earn). They also make sure that there is nothing in the film that might be offensive or illegal.

Distribution

Distribution Company

Once the film is finished, the Distribution Company makes sure it is sent out to cinemas everywhere. They make deals with chains of cinemas all over the world to make sure the film is shown. The more people see the film the more money it will make for everyone involved.

Publicity

People will only go and see the movie if they've heard about it. That's the job of the publicity company. They have to make sure the film is reviewed in newspapers and magazines to interest people and make them want to see it. They arrange for the stars to be interviewed and feed the press stories about the film before it goes into general release. Sometimes they even make up stories about the stars so that people become interested in the movie and want to see it.

Producer: Hugh McIntosh
Director: Jake Lang
Script Writer: Miranda Katz
Production Manager: Mira Seth
First Assistant Director: Jules Flynn

Director of Photography: Kyri Petros
Composer: Taro Tanaka
Production Designer: Nathalie Archer
Creative Consultant: Joe Foster

Camera Operator: Jack Roche
Focus Puller: Mark Burgess
Cam Remote: William Jones
Dollies and Cranes: Kelsie King
Grip: Ameesha Sharp
Clapper Loader: Amy Lions
Chief Lighting Technician: Matthew Emmerson
Lighting Technician: Gabriel Pitcher
Gaffer: Patrick Walsh
Best Boy Electric: Valentine Reid
Rigging Gaffer: Simon Banks

Sound Designer: Cory Little
Boom Operator: Andrew Macmillan
Sound Recordist: Joe Shamash
Foley Artist: Lisa King
Foley Mixer: Tom O'Leary

Casting Director: Anna Jones
Locations Manager: Sandro Frazzini
Props Assistant: Victoria Putler
Foreman: Pat Holt
Carpenters: Alistair Adams, Jonnie Clibbon
Construction Electrician: Pete Moss
Driver: Jill Sharpe
On-site Catering: Time for Lunch!
Costume Designer: Katy Flowers
On-set Dresser: Sarah Landeg
Make-up Artist: Larry Parker
Hairdresser: Vikram Parashar
Director of Continuity: Morris Carver